AF480522

CONTENTS

Introduction

Welcome, Barbie fans! Thank you for purchasing my second collection of Barbie clothes patterns!

In this book you will find crochet patterns of four stylish Barbie dresses. It's easy to show off your favorite Barbie doll in one of these elegant dresses, whether it's a holiday party or celebration of any special occasion.

These crochet projects are for intermediate skill level and you will learn or practice quite a few crochet stitches, depending on your crocheting experience.

I recommend using cotton yarn for Barbie dresses because it won't stretch as much and it creates a smooth look of the items. I mainly use DMC Pearl Cotton with these patterns because of its luminous colors and soft silky texture. Using the finer crochet hook, this thread is ideal to make the festive Barbie dresses!

Please refer to my video tutorials for visual illustration of stitches and techniques. You will conveniently find links to tutorials on second page of each pattern.

All four Barbie dresses are original designs by HandmadebyRaine.

Please contact me with any questions or feedback about the patterns at handmadebyraine@gmail.com.

Copyright: The patterns are for personal use only. The patterns and photos in this ebook are the property of HandmadebyRaine. You may not reproduce, redistribute or sell my patterns or claim them as your own. However, you may sell finished items made from my patterns but please refer to me as original designer and link back to my page https://handmadebyraine.com/

Thank you!

Happy crocheting!

Barbie Holiday Dress

Skill level	• Intermediate
Materials	• <u>DMC Pearl Cotton size 8</u> • 1 ball (color green in tutorial) • Ball size 49yds – 45m – 10g • Content: 100% cotton • Crochet hook 1.75 mm • Rhinestone chain • 5 tiny (1/4-inch) buttons • Stitch marker
Gauge	• 10 sc x 12 rows = 1 inch
Finished size	• about 5.5 inches long from shoulder top to bottom edge, waistband about 5 inches around.
Abbreviations US terms	• ch = chain • sc = single crochet • dc = double crochet • dc2tog = double crochet 2 together • hdc = half double crochet • flo = front loops only • blo = back loops only • sl st = slip stitch
Special stitches	• <u>dc2tog</u> = yarn over, insert hook in next st, pull up a loop, 3 loops on hook, pull through first 2 loops, yarn over, insert hook in next st, pull up a loop, 4 loops on hook, yarn over pull through first 2 loops, 3 loops on hook, yarn over, pull through 3 loops on hook.
Video tutorial	• https://youtu.be/EP0cxP4qd_A

Instructions:

Adding chain

- Ch 47.
- **Row 1** = sc in 2nd ch from hook and in each ch (46 sc).
- **Row 2** = ch 1 and turn, place rhinestone chain above 1st row stitches and sc 46 keeping the chain inside stitches (please see the video tutorial for illustration).
- **Row 3** = ch 1 and turn, sc in each st (46 sc).
- **Rows 4-9** = repeat rows 2-3.

Middle part of Dress Skirt (worked in rows)

- **Row 10** = ch 2 (doesn't count as 1st dc throughout) and turn, *dc 1 in each next 3 sc, dc2tog in next 2 sc, repeat from* until last 6 sc, dc 1 in each last 6 sc (38 dc).
- **Row 11** = ch 1 and turn, hdc in each st (38 hdc).
- **Row 12** = ch 2 and turn, dc flo in each st (38 dc).
- **Rows 13-18** = repeat rows 11-12.

Dress Top and Shoulder Straps:

- **Row 19** = ch 1 and turn, *sc 1 in each next 8 st, sc 2 in next st, repeat from*, sc 1 in each last 2 st (42 sc).
- **Rows 20-22** = ch 1 and turn, sc 1 in each st (42 sc).

Right side of top and shoulder strap:

- *ch 1 and turn, sc in each next 21 sc, repeat from* for 7 rows total (ending in center of piece).
- *ch 1 and turn, sc in each next 8 sc, repeat from* for 16 rows total.

- Fold the shoulder strap against the top edge so that last sc on strap faces the corner sc on last 21-sc row, right side remaining inside.

- Attach strap with 8 sl st, inserting hook through each stitch on strap and corresponding stitch on top edge. Fasten off, cut off thread.

Left side of top and shoulder strap:

- Join thread with sc in 1st sc on row 22, *sc in each next 21 sc.

- *ch 1 and turn, sc in each next 21 sc, repeat from* for 7 rows total (ending in center of piece).

- *ch 1 and turn, sc in each next 8 sc, repeat from* for 16 rows total.

- Fold the strap against the top edge so that last sc on strap faces 1st sc on 21-sc row, right side remaining inside, turn.

- Attach with 8 sl st, inserting hook first through st on top edge, then through corresponding st on strap. Fasten off, cut off thread.

<u>Bottom of Dress</u> (worked in rounds)

- **Round 1** = turn the piece upside down and join thread with sc in 1st foundation ch loop, sc 1 in next loop, sc 2 in next loop, *sc 1 in each next 2 loops, sc 2 in next loop, repeat from* (61 sc), sl st in 1st sc to form the round.

- **Round 2** = ch 2 (doesn't count as 1st dc), dc 1 in each sc, sl st in 1st dc.

- **Round 3** = ch 1 (doesn't count as 1st sc), sc blo in each dc, sl st in 1st sc.

- **Rounds 4-9** = repeat rounds 2-3. Fasten off, cut off thread, weave in all ends.

<u>Back Closure and Neckline</u>

<u>Back closure with 5 button loops:</u>

- Join thread with sc in bottom edge space on left side of back opening, sc in next 2 edge spaces, you can make more sc stitches if you need in order to reach the row between 3rd and 4th chain rows (it is 7th row from the very beginning), *ch 6 for button loop, sl st through sc below, sc in next 5 edge spaces, repeat from* five times, instead of last 5 sc after 5th button loop sc 3 with last sc in shoulder strap connection space. Fasten off, cut off thread.

<u>Neckline:</u>

- Join thread with sc in shoulder strap connection space on opposite side from button loops, you will work neckline sc stitches on the inside while holding the chain inside stitches, so it will display on outside.

- *sc in next 2 edge spaces, skip next space, repeat from* until the front center, sc2tog in 2 corner spaces, repeat from* until the second shoulder strap connection space. Fasten off, cut off thread and chain.

Back closure and buttons:

- Join thread with sc in upper edge space on right side of back opening where you started with chain, sc in each space along the edge. Fasten off, leave longer tail (about 15 inches) for buttons, cut off.

- Use the long tail to sew on 5 buttons. Weave in all ends.

Barbie Princess Dress

Skill level	• Intermediate
Materials	• <u>DMC Pearl Cotton size 8</u> • 1 ball blue (color A), color in tutorial Electric Blue • Ball size 49yds – 45m – 10g • <u>Liz Metallic size 20</u> • 1 ball gold (color B), color in tutorial Sand Dorllar • Ball size 155yds – 25g • Crochet hook 1.75 mm • 3x 6mm beads or tiny (1/4-inch) buttons
Gauge	• 11 sc x 13 rows = 1 inch
Finished size	• about 5.5 inches long from shoulder top to bottom edge, waist about 4 inches around
Abbreviations US terms	• ch = chain • sc = single crochet • sc2tog = single crochet 2 together • sl st = slip stitch • hdc = half double crochet • dc = double crochet
Special stitches	• <u>sc2tog</u> = insert hook in next st, pull up a loop, 2 loops on hook, insert hook in next st, pull up a loop, 3 loops on hook, yarn over and pull through 3 loops on hook.
Video tutorial	https://youtu.be/ibJF39IPOiw

Instructions:

Front Panel

- With color B ch 6.

- **Row 1** = sc in 2nd ch from hook, sc in each next 4 ch (5 sc).

- **Rows 2-15** = ch 1 and turn, sc in each sc.

- **Row 16** = ch 1 and turn, sc2tog in first 2 sc, sc in next sc, sc2tog in last 2 sc.

- **Rows 17-18** = ch and turn, sc in each sc (3 sc).

- **Row 19** = ch 1 and turn, sc2tog in first 2 st, sc2tog with first leg going in same st as last sc2tog and second leg going in last st on the row.

- **Row 20** = ch 1 and turn, sc in each 2 st.

- **Row 21** = ch 1 and turn, sc2tog in 2 st, fasten off, cut off.

Dress Top and Shoulder Straps (worked in rows)

LEFT SIDE:

- **Row 1** = join color A with sl st in upper left corner of front panel, sl st along the edge (20 sl st).

- **Row 2** = ch 1 and turn, sc in upper loop of each sl st (20 sc).

- **Rows 3-16** = ch 1 and turn, sc in each sc.

- **Row 17** = ch 15 for left shoulder strap, count 6 spaces on top edge to the left from the front panel and sl st in 6th space, also sl st in next space (5th from the front panel), turn, sc in each ch and in each next sc (35 sc).

- **Row 18** = ch 1 and turn, sc in each sc, sl st in next 2 spaces on top edge (4th and 3rd from the front panel).

- **Row 19** = turn, sc in each sc (35 sc).

- **Row 20** = ch 1 and turn, sc in each sc, sl st in next 2 spaces on top edge (2nd and 1st from the front panel).

- **Row 21** = turn, sc in each sc (35 sc).

- **Rows 22-24** = ch 1 and turn, sc in next 20 sc.

- **Row 25** = ch 1 and turn, sc in next 10 sc, sl st in next 2 sc, fasten off, cut off.

RIGHT SIDE:

- **Row 1** = join color A with sl st in right side bottom space of front panel, sl st along the edge (20 sl st).

- **Row 2** = ch 1 and turn, sc in upper loop of each sl st (20 sc).

- **Rows 3-17** = ch 1 and turn, sc in each sc.

- **Row 18** = ch 15 for right shoulder strap, count 6 spaces on top edge to the right from the front panel and sl st in 6th space, also sl st in next space (5th from the front panel), turn, sc in each ch and in each next sc (35 sc).

- **Row 19** = ch 1 and turn, sc in each sc, sl st in next 2 spaces on top edge (4th and 3rd from the front panel).

- **Row 20** = turn, sc in each sc (35 sc).

- **Row 21** = ch 1 and turn, sc in each sc, sl st in next 2 spaces on top edge (2nd and 1st from the front panel).

- **Row 22** = turn, sc in each sc (35 sc).

- **Row 23** = ch 1 and turn, sc in next 20 sc.

- **Row 24** = ch 1 and turn, sc in next 2 sc, ch 6 for first buttonloop, sl st in same sc where 6ch started, sc in each next 7 sc, ch 6 for next buttonloop, sl st in same sc where 6ch started, sl st in each next 7 sc, ch 6 for next buttonloop, sl st in same sc where 6ch started, sl st in each next 4 sc, fasten off, don't cut off.

Dress Skirt (worked in rounds)

- **1st Ruffle Round 1** = bring the top's opposite bottom corner close to the working loop, insert hook in that corner space to make 1st sc and form a ring for skirt, working the round on right side of dress sc 42 along the edge, sl st in 1st sc.

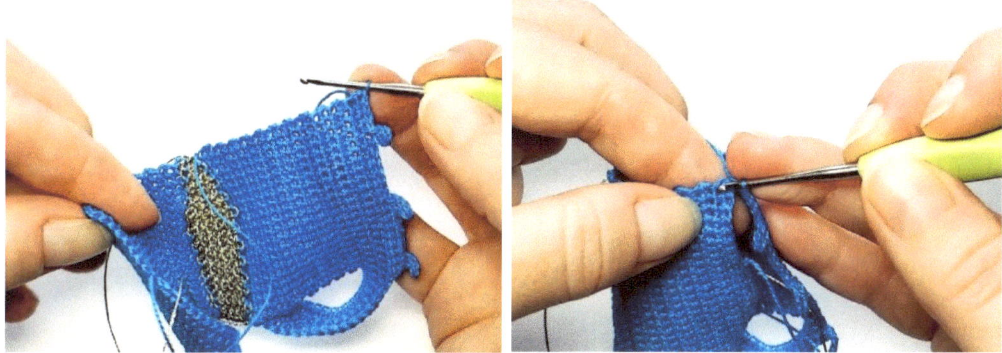

- **Round 2** = ch 1, sc in same st, *ch 2, skip next sc, sc in next sc, repeat from*, sl st in 1st sc.

- **Round 3** = sl st in first ch2-space, ch 1, sc in same space, *ch 3, sc in next ch2-space, repeat from*, instead of last 3ch = ch 1 and hdc in 1st sc.

- **Round 4** = ch 1, sc in same space, *ch 3, sc in next ch3-space, repeat from*, instead of last 3ch = ch 1 and hdc in 1st sc.

- **Round 5** = ch 1, sc in same space, *ch 3, sc in next ch3-space, repeat from*, ch 3, sl st in 1st sc, fasten off, cut off.

- **Round 6** = join color B with sc in 1st ch3-space, repeat round 5, fasten off, cut off.

- <u>**2nd Ruffle Round 1**</u> = (work this round on the wrong side of 1st ruffle) join color A with dc inserting hook from the inside in sc on round 3 of 1st ruffle, ch 1, *dc in next sc on round 3 of 1st ruffle, ch 1, repeat from*, sl st in 1st dc.

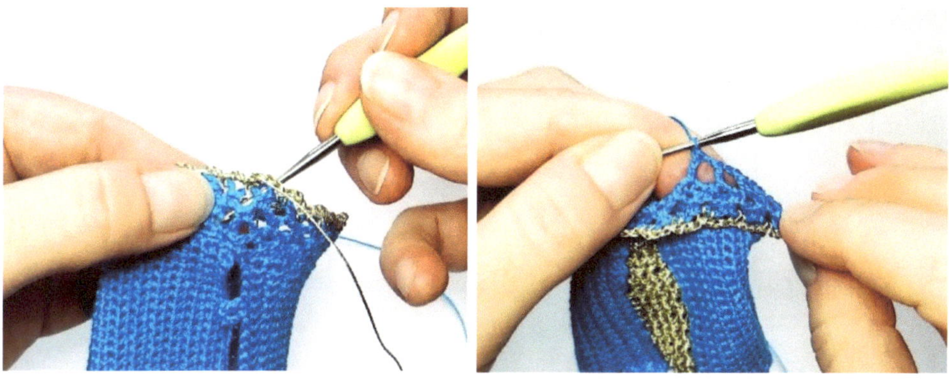

- **Round 2** = ch 1, sc in same dc, *ch 2, sc in next ch1-space, ch 2, sc in next dc, ch 3, sc in next dc, repeat from* until last ch1-space, ch 1 and hdc in 1st sc.

- **Rounds 3-4** = ch 1, sc in same space, *ch 3, sc in next ch-space, repeat from*, instead of last 3ch = ch 1 and hdc in 1st sc.

- **Round 5** = ch 1, sc in same space, *ch 3, sc in next ch3-space, repeat from*, ch 3, sl st in 1st sc, fasten off, cut off.

- **Round 6** = join color B with sc in 1st ch3-space, repeat round 5, fasten off, cut off.

- <u>3rd Ruffle Round 1</u> = (work this round on the wrong side of 2nd ruffle) join color A with dc inserting hook from the inside in sc on round 3 of 2nd ruffle, ch 1, *dc in next sc on round 3 of 2nd ruffle, ch 1, repeat from*, sl st in 1st dc.

- **Round 2** = sl st in next ch1-space, ch 1, sc, *ch 3, sc in next ch1-space, repeat from*, instead of last 3ch = ch 1 and hdc in 1st sc.

- **Rounds 3-4** = ch 1, sc in same space, *ch 3, sc in next ch3-space, repeat from*, instead of last 3ch = ch 1 and hdc in 1st sc.

- **Round 5** = ch 1, sc in same space, *ch 3, sc in next ch3-space, repeat from*, ch 3, sl st in 1st sc, fasten off, cut off.

- **Round 6** = join color B with sc in 1st ch3-space, repeat round 5, fasten off, cut off.

- <u>Ruffles 4-6</u> = repeat Ruffle 3.

<u>Sleeves</u> (worked in rows)

- **Row 1** = skip 1 st on shoulder strap's 1st row and join color A with sc in next st, *ch 3, skip next sc, sc in next sc, repeat from* (6 ch3-spaces), until last st on shoulder strap.

- **Row 2** = sc in that last st, turn, *ch 3, sc in next ch3-space, repeat from*, end the row with sc in 1st skipped st on shoulder strap (7 ch3-spaces), fasten off, cut off.

- **Row 3** = join color B with sl st in space right under the last sc of row 2, *ch 3, sc in next ch3-space, repeat from*, end the row with sl st in space under 1st sc of row 2 (8 ch3-spaces), fasten off, cut off.

- Weave in all ends.

Beads or Buttons

- Sew on 3 beads or buttons on right side of back opening to match the buttonloops on left side.

Cross Stitches

- Using fine sewing needle and color A make cross stitches on front panel:

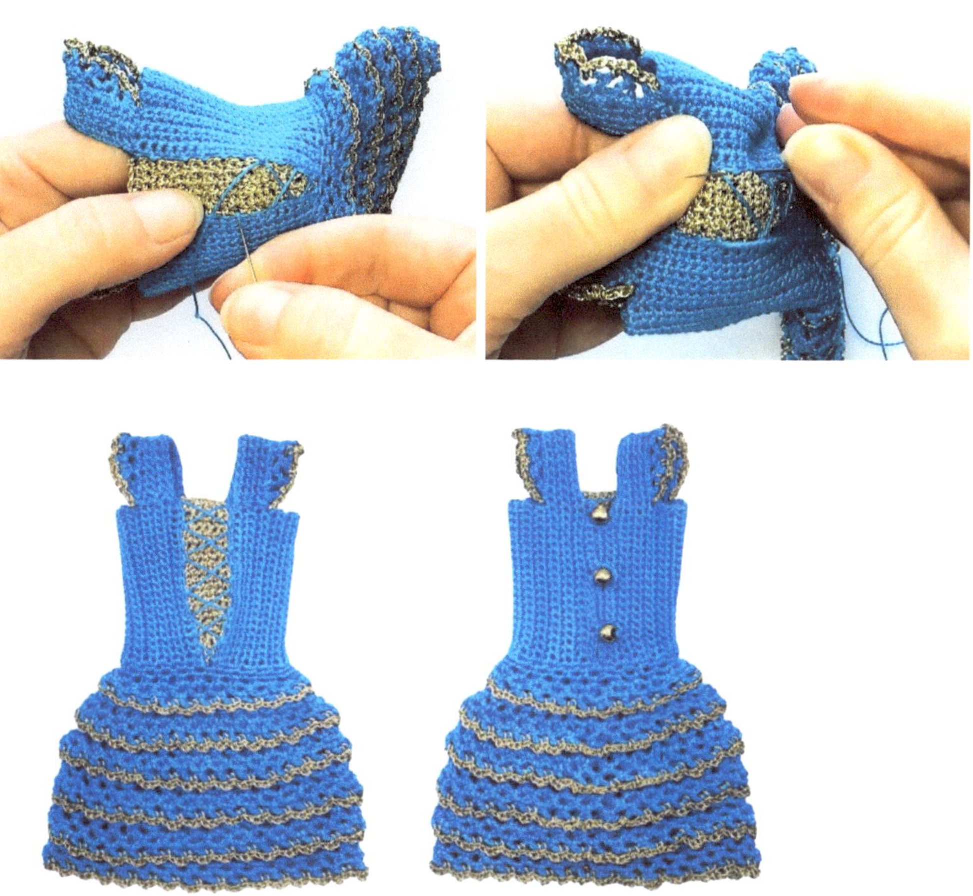

Barbie Vogue Dress

Skill level	• Intermediate
Materials	• <u>Aunt Lydia's crochet thread size 3</u> • 1 ball red (color A), 1 ball black (color B) • Ball size 150 yds – 137 m • Content: 100% cotton • Crochet hook 2.75 mm • Crochet hook 1.5 mm for beads • 3 beads size 2/0 or tiny buttons • Stitch marker
Gauge	• 5 esc x 5 rows = 1 inch
Finished size	• about 5.5 inches long from shoulder top to bottom edge, waistband about 5 inches around.
Abbreviations US terms	• ch = chain • esc = extended single crochet • sc = single crochet • sl st = slip stitch
Special stitches	• <u>esc</u> = insert hook in indicated stitch, pull up a loop, yarn over, pull through first loop on hook, yarn over, pull through two remaining loops on hook. • <u>spike stitch</u> = insert hook in space below next sc on previous round, yarn over, pull up long loop, yarn over, pull through 2 loops.
Video tutorial	• https://youtu.be/gGjZEY4-GJM

Instructions:

<u>Dress Top</u> (worked in rows, starts with 1st sleeve and ends with 2nd sleeve)

- *Starting first sleeve*: with color A (leave 15-inch tail for stitching later) ch 11.
- **Row 1** = esc in 2nd ch from hook, esc in each next ch (10 esc).
- **Rows 2-6** = ch 1 and turn, esc 1 in each st. *First sleeve completed.*
- **Row 7** = ch 9, esc in 2nd ch from hook, esc in each next 7 ch, esc in each next 10 st, ch 9.
- **Row 8** = esc in 2nd ch from hook, esc in each next 7 ch, esc in each next st (26 esc).
- **Rows 9-11** = ch 1 and turn, esc 1 in each st.
- **Row 12** = ch and turn, esc 1 in each next 8 stitches, ch 19 *(= neck and back opening)*.
- **Row 13** = esc in 2nd ch from hook, esc in each next 17 ch, esc in each next st (26 esc).
- **Rows 14-16** = ch 1 and turn, esc 1 in each st.
- **Row 17** = ch and turn, esc 1 in each next 18 st (leave last 8 st unworked). *Second sleeve started.*
- **Row 18** = ch 1 and turn, esc 1 in each next 10 st.
- **Rows 19-23** = ch 1 and turn, esc 1 in each st, fasten off, cut off color A leaving 15-inch tail for stitching later. *Second sleeve completed.*
- Fold the piece in half to have esc rows running vertically.
- Using needle and long tail stitch the sides together and turn the piece right side out.

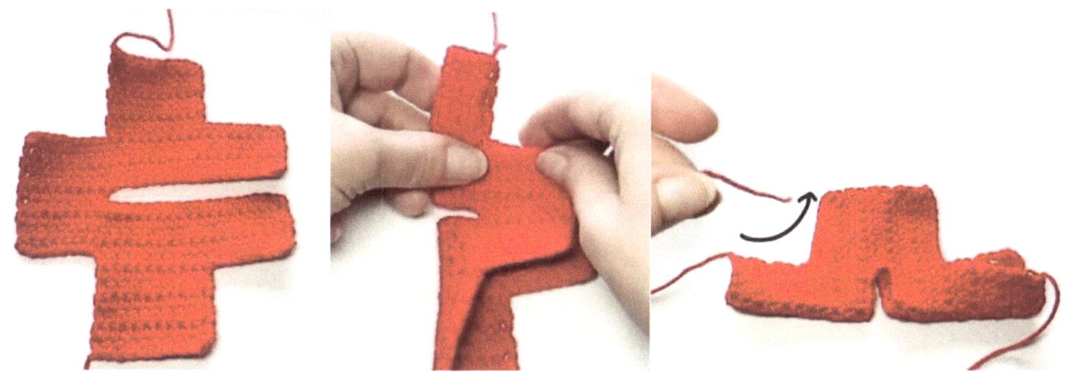

<u>Dress Skirt</u> (worked in rounds)

- **Round 1** = holding the top same way as on 3rd photo above, except facing the back side opening (= turn it horizontally from the photo position) join color B with sc in end space of first row, sc in end space of each row (19 sc), sl st in 1st sc to form a ring.

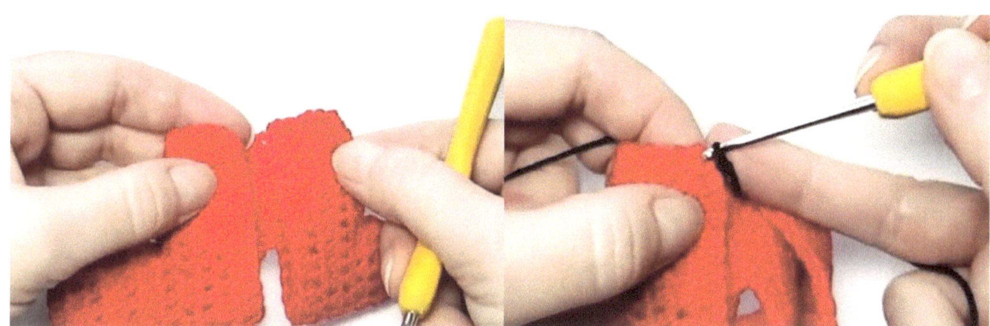

- **Round 2** = ch 1, sc 2 in each sc (38 sc), sl st in 1st sc, pull the loop longer and leave it inside the work, don't cut off.

- **Round 3** = Join color A with sc in 1st sc, spike st in next sc, *sc in next sc, spike st in next sc, repeat from*, sl st in 1st sc.

- **Round 4** = ch 1, sc in each st, sl st in 1st sc, pull the loop longer and leave it inside the work.

- **Round 5** = insert hook through 1st sc, then through color B loop and pull it through sc, yarn over and pull through loop on hook (=1st sc), spike st in next sc, *sc in next sc, spike st in next sc, repeat from*, sl st in 1st sc.

- **Round 6** = ch 1, sc in each st, sl st in 1st sc, pull the loop longer and leave it inside the work.

- **Rounds 7-20** = repeat rounds 5 and 6 changing colors after each 2 rounds; after round 20 fasten off, cut off color A.

- **Round 21** = with color B repeat round 5.

- **Round 22** = ch 1, sc in 1st sc, *ch 1, skip next st, sc in next sc, repeat from*, sl st in 1st sc, fasten off, cut off color B.

Back Closure & Neck Opening

- Join color A with sl st in bottom st of back opening left side, inserting hook in 1st st of top's last row, sl st in next st, ch 4 for 1st buttonloop, insert hook through 1st ch and space on edge where 4ch started, yarn over and pull through all loops on hook, (sl st in each next 2 st, ch 4 for next buttonloop, sl st inserting hook through 1st ch and st where 4ch started) twice, sl st in each next st along neckline until front center.

- Sl st 2 in center space of neckline, sl st in each next st until 7 stitches on the other side of edge on the back (you can insert stitch marker in that 7th st, this is where the 1st bead will go).

- Sl st in marked 7th st, (take hook out of working loop, insert finer hook through the bead, then through the working loop and pull it through the bead, switch back to bigger hook, sl st inserting hook through esc below the bead, sl st in each next 2 st) twice, add the 3rd bead same way, sl st in last 2 st, sl st one more inserting hook through the stitch on color B round below. Fasten off, cut off color A. Weave in all ends.

Barbie Skirt Dress and Purse

Skill level	• Intermediate
Materials	• <u>DMC Pearl Cotton size 5</u> • 1 ball black or navy blue (color A), 1 ball white (color B) • Ball size 49yds – 45m – 10g • Content: 100% cotton • Crochet hook 2.75 mm • Crochet hook 2 mm for beads • 4x 6mm beads, 18x 4mm beads • Stitch marker
Gauge	• 8 hdc x 5 rows = 1 inch
Finished size	• Dress: about 5 inches long from shoulder top to bottom edge, waistband about 4.5 inches around. • Purse: height about 0.75 inches, width about 1.75 inches.
Abbreviations US terms	• ch = chain • sc = single crochet • beg = beginning • hdc = half double crochet • sl st = slip stitch • esc = extended single crochet
Special stitches	• esc = insert hook in indicated stitch, pull up a loop, yarn over, pull through one loop on hook, yarn over, pull through two remaining loops on hook.
Video tutorial	• Barbie outfit https://youtu.be/8Ev9z5H0jbQ • Magic ring https://youtu.be/CV9wQZAjSgc

Instructions:

Dress Skirt

Start with waistband – it is worked in rows:

- With color A ch 25.

- **Row 1** = sc in 2nd ch from hook and in each next ch (24 sc).

- **Rows 2-4** = ch 1, turn, sc 1 in each st (24 sc).

Skirt is worked in rounds:

- **Round 5** = ch 1, bring up the other end of waistband to form a ring, inserting hook in beg 1st sc of row 4 *hdc 1 in each next 3 sc, hdc 2 in next sc, repeat from*, end the round with 2 hdc in last sc (30 hdc), sl st in 1st hdc.

- **Round 6** = ch 1, *hdc 1 in each next 4 st, hdc 2 in next st, repeat from*, end the round with 2 hdc in last st, sl st in 1st hdc.

- **Round 7** = ch 1, *hdc 1 in each next 5 st, hdc 2 in next st, repeat from*, end the round with 2 hdc in last st, sl st in 1st hdc.

- **Round 8** = ch 1, *hdc 1 in each next 6 st, hdc 2 in next st, repeat from*, end the round with 2 hdc in last st, sl st in 1st hdc.

- **Rounds 9-15** = repeat the increasing pattern, on each round you will have 1 more hdc before increasing in the next st (R9 = hdc1 in 7 st, hdc2 in 8th st), on last 15th round hdc1 in 13 st and hdc2 in 14th st.

- **Edge** = sl st in each hdc, sl st in 1st st, fasten off, cut off color A.

Dress Top (worked in rows)

- **Row 1** = join color B with esc in first space between 2 foundation chains on waistband, esc 1 more in same space, *skip next space between foundation chains, esc 2 in next space, repeat from* until last space, esc 2 in last space (26 esc).

- **Row 2** = ch 1 and turn, (esc 1 in each next 5 st, esc 2 in next st) repeat 4 times, esc 1 in each last 2 st (30 esc).

- **Rows 3-8** = ch 1 and turn, esc 1 in each st (30 esc), at end of 8th row don't cut off thread.

Sleeves

- Turn, sl st in next st (sleeve starts in 2nd st), ch 10, skip 10 st on last row of dress top, sl st in next st.

- **Row 1** = turn, sl st in 1st skipped sc inside sleeve hole, sc 1 in each 10 ch, sl st in each next 2 st on last row of top. Make sure to sl st inside sleeve hole, not on the other side of sleeve.

- **Row 2** = turn, sc 1 in each 10 sc, sl st in each next 2 st inside sleeve hole.

- **Row 3** = turn, sc 1 in each 10 sc, sl st in next st, leave 4 remaining stitches on last row of top inside sleeve hole unworked.

- **Rows 4-6** = turn, sc 1 in each 10 sc, sl st in same st where the last sl st of previous row was made (not in the next st). After 6th row fasten off, cut off thread.

- Work 2nd sleeve facing the inside of top, join color B with sl st in 2nd st on the opposite side of top's last row, ch 10, skip 10, sl st in next st.

- Repeat rows 1-6 of the first sleeve. Weave in all color B thread ends, keep the beg color A thread tail for stitching later.

Back Closure

- **Right side with beads** – using 2 mm crochet hook join color B with sl st in top's last row st next to sleeve, sl st 2 in corner space.

- Attaching beads - (take hook out of working loop, insert it through the bead and pull working loop through the bead, sl st 6 in side space of esc rows) twice, add 3rd bead same way, sl st 2 in side of 1st row of waistband, fasten off, cut off thread.

- **Left side with loops** – join color B with sl st in space of 1st waistband row where the 1st esc started.

- Ch 6, to make a button loop insert hook through 6th ch from hook and same space where you joined color B, yarn over and pull through all loops on hook, (sl st 6 in side space of esc rows, ch 6, insert hook through 6th ch from hook and space on the base of ch-6, yarn over and pull through all loops on hook) twice, sl st in corner of edge, sl st in upper edge next to sleeve, fasten off, cut off thread.

- Weave in all remaining ends, use beg color A tail to adjust the size of waistband hole.

<u>Purse</u> (worked in continuous rounds)

- With 2.75 mm hook and color B make a magic ring (please see video tutorial, link on 2nd page).

- **Round 1** = sc 8 in the ring, place stitch marker in 1st sc.

- **Round 2** = sc 2 in each st (16 sc), move the stitch marker into the 1st st on this round (if you prefer).

- **Round 3** = *sc 1 in next st, sc 2 in next st, repeat from* (24 sc).

- **Round 4** = *sc 1 in each next 2 st, sc 2 in next st, repeat from* (32 sc).

- **Round 5** = *sc 1 in each next 3 st, sc 2 in next st, repeat from* (40 sc).

- **Round 6** = (sc 1 in each next 4 st, sc 2 in next st) seven times, instead of last 4sc + 2sc just sc 1 in each next 3.

- Fold the piece in two, insert hook through next sc and corresponding st on opposite side, yarn over and pull through both sides and loop on hook.

- Ch 12 (first handle), skip 6 st on both side, sl st in next st inserting hook through both sides.

- Continue down the second side of purse - sl st 8 inserting hook through both sides until bottom corner, fasten off, cut off thread.

- Join thread with sl st on the other side in bottom corner, inserting hook through both sides sl st 7 through both sides until the handle.

- Sl st in same st where 1st handle started, ch 12 (second handle), sl st in same st where 1st handle was attached with sl st.

- Fasten off, cut off thread. Using the last thread tail and sewing needle attach 6 mm bead in center stitch under purse opening.

- Weave in remaining ends.

www.ingramcontent.com/pod-product-compliance
Lightning Source LLC
Chambersburg PA
CBHW042017110726
48006CB00004B/1117